Original title:
Tales from the Christmas Tree

Copyright © 2024 Creative Arts Management OÜ
All rights reserved.

Author: William Hawthorne
ISBN HARDBACK: 978-9916-94-382-3
ISBN PAPERBACK: 978-9916-94-383-0

The Tradition of Togetherness

Gathered 'round with hats askew,
A feast of snacks we always brew.
The dog steals ham, the cat is sly,
As chaos reigns, we laugh and sigh.

Each year a puzzle, just one piece,
The ornament drops, we all cease.
With jokes and jabs, the stories flow,
United in mirth, our love does grow.

Echoing Laughter in the Cold

Snowflakes fall like little pranks,
We slip and slide, giving thanks.
Hot cocoa spills on the old man's shoe,
He grumbles low, then laughs anew.

The carolers sing slightly off-key,
As we peek out, it's fun to see.
With voices raised, we make a sound,
In this frozen joy, true warmth is found.

The Harmony of Holiday Lights

Twinkling bulbs, a sight to behold,
The cat gets tangled, oh so bold.
The neighbors glare at our glowing flair,
While we just chuckle, without a care.

The mismatched colors, a rainbow's laugh,
We start a dance, take a silly half.
With sparkling cheer lighting the night,
In a glow of joy, everything feels right.

Embracing Nostalgic Nights

Old photos shared, we tease and jest,
Of grandma's fruitcake, we confess.
The stories told of years gone by,
As laughter bubbles, we can't deny.

The gift wrap fights, a paper war,
We tumble, giggle, then ask for more.
With dreams of youth, we feel so bright,
Embracing friendship on this night.

Tinsel Dreams Unwrapped

Beneath the lights, a cat took flight,
Chasing the tinsel, oh what a sight!
Spinning and leaping with glee in the air,
Knocking down ornaments without a care.

Dad screams in fright, but laughter abounds,
Mom giggles softly at the clatter of sounds.
The tree shakes and quakes, like a dance so wild,
As Uncle Joe's belly wobbles, just like a child.

Glow of Timeless Nights

Grandpa's old sweater—it's bright and it's bold,
With reindeer that dance, it's a sight to behold!
  He prances around, singing loud off-key,
  While the dog looks at him as if to agree.

Lights flicker and flash, it's a chaos of cheer,
As Aunt Sue declares, 'I'll bring out the beer!'
With laughter and joy filling up every space,
'Tis the season for fun—not a moment to waste!

Beneath the Boughs

Under the branches, the kids all conspire,
To build a fort made of pillows and fire!
They giggle and giggle, then hide from the sight,
While Dad trips on wrappers, oh what a fright!

With cookies all crumbled and milk spilled anew,
It looks like a war happened just between two!
But soon there's a truce in the laughter-filled din,
As they all unite to see who can win.

Frosted Stories in the Attic

Up in the attic, old treasures await,
A box of big hats and a toy pirate crate.
Mom tries on a hat that's floppy and bright,
While Dad acts like Captain with all of his might!

Then out comes the snowman, a mess on the floor,
With googly eyes that are ready to score.
They topple and tumble in laughter and cheer,
Who knew the attic could hold so much dear?

Welcome to the Wonder

In the corner stands a cheer,
Lights are twinkling, oh so near.
Cats are plotting, tails are high,
While ornaments all start to fly.

Tinsel tangled in the dog,
He just smiles, like a log.
Sparkling star upon the top,
Will it stay there? Hop, hop, hop!

Memories Wrapped in Garlands

Baking cookies, sprinkle fight,
Flour dancing in the light.
Grandma's recipes, secrets shared,
Burnt a batch? No one dared!

Pine needles stuck in the rugs,
Cousins dropped the mugs like thugs.
Laughter echoes, joy abounds,
As gifts get tossed on the grounds!

The Narrative of Noble Fir

Noble Fir with limbs outstretched,
Wonders of the past etched.
Squirrels sneaking, trying to munch,
On candies hidden in the bunch.

Who wrapped gifts with duct tape,
Thinking they'd make quite a shape?
All that's left is a giant mess,
But oh, what fun, we must confess!

Snowflakes and Stories

Snowflakes dance, a wild show,
Kids outside, making snow.
Then inside, warm cups of cheer,
Tales of mishaps, loud and clear.

The dog dressed up, what a sight,
He shakes off snow, such delight.
Candles flicker, stories weave,
A festive night we won't believe!

Tales of Tinsel and Time

Once a squirrel climbed up high,
With a glittery star, oh my!
He slipped on a bauble, what a sight,
Spinning like a top, oh what a fright!

The cat looked on with great dismay,
As he watched his friend's ballet sway.
Christmas cheer in a slip and a slide,
Squirrel and tinsel, a wild ride!

The Glow of Winter's Heart

Bright bulbs went blink, a dance at the door,
Caroling cats had come to explore.
With ribbons and bows stuck to their tails,
Their meows turned to jingles; what epic fails!

One feisty feline planned to impress,
But landed in wrapping, oh what a mess!
The family howled with laughter and cheer,
As their Christmas lights blinked, loud and clear!

Midnight Under the Mistletoe

At midnight, the dog had a grand plan,
To sneak a kiss from the elf-made man.
He leaped for the mistletoe in delight,
But crashed through the garland, oh what a sight!

Laughter erupted, and spirits were bright,
As he wiggled and rattled, trying to take flight.
The elf just chuckled, his cheeks all aglow,
'Tis the season for laughter, don't you know?'

Fables in Frosted Lights

A penguin once dreamt of a snowy night,
Decorating with candy canes, what a fright!
He tangled the strings, left and right,
Turning his home into a hilarious sight.

His friends gathered 'round for a giggle or two,
As he danced on the floor, a clown in a zoo.
With frosting and sprinkles, they cheered and they glowed,
Tales of their shenanigans, happily flowed!

The Winter's Tale Unfolds

In a cozy nook, a squirrel did dance,
Stole a candy cane, missed his chance.
With a jig and a spin, he took to flight,
Flew past the lights, out of sheer delight.

The cat plotted schemes, eyes all aglow,
Pounced on the gifts, but oh, what a show!
Wrapped in paper, he slipped and he slid,
As laughter erupted from all that he did.

Glimmers Amongst the Fir

A tree stood tall in the corner so bright,
Adorned with baubles that sparkled with light.
An elf on the shelf, with a grin and a wink,
Made faces at kids, all while they would blink.

The dog found the cookie, a sweet little treat,
Devoured it whole, with a gleam in his beat.
He licked his own paws, happy and proud,
While the family giggled, and laughter rang loud.

Echoes in the Soft Glow

Beneath the branches, a treasure was found,
A gnome with a laugh that echoed around.
He juggled the ornaments, two, three, then four,
Till he crashed on the floor with a loud, joyful roar.

A snowman outside, with a scarf made of flair,
Stood guard at the door, with a bit of a scare.
He waved with a twig, stole a carrot for fun,
As the kids built a snowball to send him on the run.

Wishes Carved in Wood

A wooden reindeer, with a splintered nose,
Whispered funny tales of how he once froze.
He dreamed of flying, of dashing with glee,
While the children chuckled, "That's just not for thee!"

A nutcracker stood, with a grin and a shimmy,
Laughed at his friends, when they looked just so dimmy.
With a crack and a pop, he joined in the cheer,
As the room filled with giggles, spread warmth like a beer.

Grateful Gatherings Under Stars

Underneath the twinkling lights,
We gather for our silly fights.
Uncle Joe hides in the wreath,
Scaring kids with a false belief.

Cousin Lily spills her drink,
Even Santa starts to wink.
The cat leaps onto the tree,
As grandma shouts, "Let it be!"

Laughter echoes in the night,
As we munch on cookies, just right.
Mom's burnt pie, we all agree,
Could be used as a new frisbee!

With each present, giggles grow,
What's this? A sock? Oh, the woe!
In this merry, jolly cheer,
Grateful hearts are gathered here.

A Medley of Yuletide Memories

Beneath the mistletoe we pause,
To snap a pic with Santa Claus.
Cousin Fred thinks he can sing,
A jolly tune that makes us cringe.

A goat in the yard does the dance,
While we all give it a chance.
Grandpa's glasses, now askew,
Claims he's got a clear view.

Gifts wrapped up with tape so thick,
Dad's still searching for that trick.
A sweater with reindeer so bright,
How it fits? What a fright!

The joyous noise and cheerful shouts,
Christmas joy is what it's about.
As memories fill the night sky,
We'll laugh at what brings a sigh.

An Ode Beneath the Boughs

Under branches, bright and spry,
We play games that make us cry.
The dog steals all the treats,
While grandpa snores through all the beats.

Tinsel tangled in my hair,
A festive look, beyond compare.
Laughter erupts with each gift torn,
Oh look! A hat that's way too worn!

Uncle's jokes make us groan loud,
Yet we cherish our silly crowd.
The fruitcake hardens like a rock,
Yet mom insists, "It's the shock!"

Through the giggles, joy remains,
As we dance through windowpanes.
Here beneath the boughs, we see,
Happiness is our decree.

The Evergreen Chronicles

In the corner, the cat has a plan,
With a leap and a pounce, she's lost in the span.
She swats at the baubles, how do they spin?
All her feline dreams start to begin.

The lights twinkle brightly, a dazzling show,
Yet one little bulb has a mind of its own, you know.
It flickers and flashes, a disco delight,
Even the ornaments start dancing tonight.

Grandpa's old sweater, it's red with a flair,
Next to the tree, it's a sight: quite rare!
With tinsel adorning his big furry chest,
We can't help but giggle; it's truly the best.

Cookies abound, but there's one missing treat,
A cookie thief strikes, oh the sneaky defeat!
The crumbs left behind are proof of his crime,
We laugh as we chase him—it's holiday time!

Secrets in the Sparkle

A star on the top, but it's mostly askew,
The dog's taken over, he just couldn't blew!
With ornaments falling, yet cheers in the air,
It's a festive disaster, and we don't have a care.

Candy canes clashing in culinary fights,
Sweets on the table, oh what a delight!
One sneaky sibling claims, "I'll take them all,"
As we burst into laughter, he's made such a haul.

Under the branches, a treasure we find,
Presents for everyone, oh what's the surprise?
But the real jokes linger in cards quite ornate,
With silly old poems, the humor won't wait.

As carols are sung, with a twist and a laugh,
The tree shakes and shimmies, it's a merry craft.
We raise up our glasses and toast to the night,
With every funny story, the mood feels just right!

Echoes of Holiday Cheer

A snowman outside smiles with a wink,
But he's really quite jealous of the warm drink.
Hot cocoa in hand, with marshmallows galore,
We giggle and sip, then we cheer for some more.

Ribbons and bows tied with the greatest care,
But then Uncle Joe trips—oh, who's aware?
Presents go flying, laughter fills the room,
We declare it a moment where joy starts to bloom.

The tree is a wonder, with gifts piled high,
But watch for the toddler; he's aiming to fly.
With his sights on the goodies, oh what a quest,
He stumbles and giggles, it's all quite a jest.

With eggnog for all, and cookies galore,
We reminisce tales of the years gone before.
The echoes of laughter ring clear and bright,
This holiday magic, a pure sheer delight!

A Gathering of Wishes

The kids chase each other, what a wild sight,
As they sneak 'round the tree, giggling with delight.
With whispers of secrets, they huddle so tight,
Each wish on their lips shines like stars in the night.

A present for Mom, wrapped up with such care,
But Dad swipes a cookie, with crumbs in his hair!
The mischief afoot leads to giggly fights,
As we gather 'round, it's a scene filled with light.

The lights cast shadows that sway like a dance,
As Aunt Sally tries juggling; oh, what a chance!
Two ornaments tumble, we gasp and we cheer,
For each little mishap brings joy and good cheer.

With laughter and love filling up every space,
Our hearts are entwined in this magical place.
So raise up a toast to the whims that unfold,
In this gathering of wishes, our stories told.

The Magic Within the Mantle

On the mantle, socks hang tight,
Each one hoping for a good night.
Rats in red suits, they plan their heist,
Snatching treats, oh how they're spiced!

Santa's sleigh breaks down for glee,
As the reindeer sip cocoa with great esprit.
A yogurt spill winds up the tale,
As Rudolph sneezes, they all turn pale!

Cozy Corners and Cinnamon Wishes

In cozy corners, cats conspire,
To unravel lights, they're always a flyer.
Cinnamon rolls on the plate wait,
As the mouse is plotting a sneaky fate!

Cookies with sprinkles, all round and sweet,
But one brave chipmunk claims his retreat.
He nibbles a treat, oh what a bite,
While the dog just snores, dreaming of flight!

Underneath the Twinkling Skies

Underneath the twinkling glow,
The kids set traps for a cheeky crow.
With breadcrumbs scattered and giggles loud,
They wait in joy, a playful crowd!

A squirrel pops in for a grand feast,
While the cat just thinks he's the least.
Jumping on branches, they all act spry,
As the moonlight winks and says hi!

The Silent Choir of Baubles

The baubles sing in silent cheer,
As the cat climbs high, spreading fear.
A daring leap, a crash and a clang,
And down the tree, all the treasures dang!

Each ornament laughs, struck with glee,
A shimmery dance; how can this be?
While the star rolls down with a twist,
Grabbing the cat into a dizzying mist!

A Pine-scented Reverie

Under the boughs, a squirrel snickers,
As ornaments sway like drunken flickers.
The star on top has seen better days,
It's lopsided, but who really pays?

With each tinsel tease, a cat darts,
Knocking down baubles, breaking hearts.
The smell of pine fills up the air,
Unwrapping gifts turns into a dare.

Cousin Joe brings fruitcake wrapped tight,
It gleams like a rock in broad daylight.
We chuckle as he takes a big bite,
His face screams 'help' — what a funny sight.

Laughter echoes around the room,
While Aunt Edna's trousers start to loom.
The pine-scented chaos, pure delight,
Is what makes our holiday nights bright.

Flickering Lights, Fading Hours

Strings of lights in tangled masses,
Create a disco with blinking passes.
The dog barks at shadows on the wall,
While Grandpa's snoring steals the hall.

Each flicker tells a tale of glee,
Of Christmas past and the spilled eggnog spree.
Mom frowns as the lights start to blink,
'Is it a party or just time to drink?'

We gather 'round with mugs in hand,
While Uncle Bob makes brownies grand.
He shrieks with glee, the oven's hot,
'Who needs a timer? This is the spot!'

As hours fade in a merry twist,
Each moment a memory we can't resist.
Through giggles and joy, the night spins fast,
With flickering lights, we have a blast.

Echoes of a Winter's Glow

Winter whispers with each gusty breeze,
Echoing tales of mischief with ease.
The snowman's eyes, two rocks that glare,
He's got a scarf, but does he care?

Children sleigh ride down the hill,
With laughter loud, they can't sit still.
A snowball flies, a strategic throw,
Right at Grandma, what a lovely show!

In the glow of lights, a dance breaks free,
Each wobble matched with wild glee.
The cookies vanish in a blink,
As sneaky hands grab and wink.

With echoes ringing through the night,
Laughter and warmth make everything right.
Though winter's chill bites at our toes,
In this joyful chaos, love always grows.

The Hidden Gifts of the Season

Beneath the tree, odd gifts do hide,
A puppy barks, with joy and pride.
Mismatched socks and ties so bright,
What's grandma thinking? She's a delight!

Wrapped in glitter, surprises untold,
An empty box, or so I'm told.
What's inside? A mystery grand!
It's like a treasure map unplanned.

With each unwrapping, giggles arise,
As Dad retrieves worst Christmas buys.
A singing fish, what a sight indeed,
Makes us howl; it's just what we need.

The season's gifts, both silly and true,
Bring laughter and joy to me and you.
In this merry mess, love's the key,
And that's the best gift, surely you'll agree.

The Heart of the Hearth

In the corner, a squirrel's caught,
Nibbling nuts that he forgot.
Grandpa's snoring, loud as can be,
Dreaming of cookies, hilariously free.

The cat eyes the ornaments with glee,
Pouncing now, as spry as can be.
Uncle Joe laughs, and spills his drink,
While Aunt Sue rolls her eyes in a blink.

Twinkling lights play tricks on the dog,
Chasing shadows like a clumsy frog.
All the laughter fills up the air,
Joyful chaos, with love everywhere.

Radiance in the Room

The glow of the lights makes us all squint,
Uncle Bob's tie is quite the hint.
He's wearing it backward, what a sight!
Our holiday dinner is pure delight.

Grandma's knitting, with yarn in a twist,
Creating a sweater no one wants, missed.
While cousin Timmy tries on a hat,
That looks like a mushroom, imagine that!

Laughter erupts, as we gather 'round,
Each goofy story makes hearts pound.
The warmth of the room, the joy we share,
While the tree stands proudly, in glittering flare.

Wishes Clad in Evergreen

A wish on a branch, lost in the fray,
Falling right off, much to our dismay.
The dog runs past, in a blur of fur,
Snatching the gift meant for her.

The stockings are stuffed, but look very odd,
Filled with candy and socks; could it be fraud?
Dad's trying to hide the new strange gift,
While mom just giggles, giving him a lift.

The candles flicker, the shadows they tease,
As we all try to settle, enjoying the breeze.
With every crackling sound, laughter unfurls,
In the midst of the chaos, our joy twirls.

Hushed Voices in the Glow

Under the tree, whispers take flight,
As kids plot the ultimate surprise at night.
Tinsel flies high like a well-aimed dart,
While giggles escape from the depths of their heart.

Uncle Pete sneezes, a glorious blast,
Santa's beard flies off, what a contrast!
Mom shakes her head, can't help but giggle,
As we sit back, struggling not to wiggle.

The wrapping paper turns into a war,
With paper balls flying, oh what a score!
As laughter erupts, we let our hearts sing,
In the glow of the tree, joy is the king.

When Frost Meets the Flame

Once Frost danced with a flaming spirit,
Their zigzagging moves made all the kids merit.
Hot cocoa spilled as the giggles took flight,
Even the snowmen were laughing all night.

Frost whispered jokes to the nearby pine,
With needles that tickled, they both crossed a line.
Fire responded with a blazing bright grin,
Who knew winter could party so thin?

Muffins would burn, the cookies went pop,
Each time they frolicked, the mess never stopped.
Even the sleigh bells began to chime,
Frost and Flame found their rhythm sublime.

So next holiday, if you hear a cheer,
Know Frost is near and so is the beer!
Together they'll dance, to the world's delight,
Causing a ruckus from evening till night.

A Dream in Twelve Days

On the first day, a partridge sang low,
But the tree sighed softly; it wanted to grow.
On the second, two turtles confused their shells,
Spinning like tops, those festive little elves.

Three French hens flapped, caught in a twine,
Their chaos exploded, an egg-shaped design.
Four calling birds sang songs off-key,
Shaking the neighbors, 'Do we need to flee?'

Five golden rings? That's a tire, you see!
The dog thought it was a new kind of tree.
Six geese a-laying, but they forgot where,
Dropping their eggs with no ounce of care.

Seven swans started to glide about,
Hit a ceiling fan—oh, was there a shout?
On the final day, laughter took the stage,
Twelve days passed in an ornate, warm cage.

Ornaments of Hope

A shiny red bulb, its smile was bright,
Nodding with charm from morning till night.
A blue one yelled, "Can I light up the end?"
As they giggled and spun, whom would they offend?

The tinsel all giggled, so shiny and proud,
As they wrapped themselves round, drawing quite a crowd.
With laughter, they tangled each ball in a cheer,
Hoping the humans would not shed a tear.

But one little elf slipped, fell on the floor,
As ornaments chuckled, "We're tough to ignore!"
They joined in the mayhem, spreading the cheer,
Hope was the theme, loud and clear through their sneer.

"More fun, less fuss!" they yelled in a spree,
"We're not here for drama, just laughter's decree!"
The holiday came and went with a roar,
Thanks to those ornaments, comedy galore.

Shadows of Celebration

Under the tree, shadows jumped with glee,
They played silly games, as cheeky as could be.
One shadow was a nutcracker, legs all akimbo,
While another spun tales, bright as a rainbow.

The star on top tried to keep it all straight,
But all of their antics just tempted the fate.
"Let's dance in the dark!" the shadows all yelled,
Creating a ruckus, with giggles they meld.

A shadow of Santa slipped, tripped on a sleigh,
While Mrs. Claus chortled and shouted,
"Hip-hip-hooray!"
The more that they laughed, the brighter they shone,
Like flickering lights, they danced 'round alone.

So if you look close, under twinkling lights,
You might catch a glimpse of their marvelous sights.
In the shadows of joy, let your laughter resound,
For holiday cheer is where love can be found.

Layers of Laughter and Light

On branches high, a sock did cling,
A cat in stealth, prepared to spring.
The ornaments danced with silly cheer,
While grandma searched for lost eggnog beer.

The lights flickered, a disco ball,
Uncle Joe tripped, and took a fall.
The gingerbread men ran for the door,
Chased by kids, they wanted more!

Pine needles stuck to the holiday pie,
As Aunt Meg laughed and wondered why.
The laughter echoed, a catchy tune,
While the tinsel sparkled, a glittering boon.

So gather 'round the tree so bright,
With stories that bring sheer delight.
Each layer of joy wrapped with care,
In this merry mess, we share and flare.

The Painter's Colour Palette

Oh, what a sight, the colors glue!
A mess of paint, what did we do?
Red and green on the cat's white fur,
Painted reindeer? More like a blur!

The kids dipped brushes, a rainbow spree,
Turned each ornament into a bee.
The star up top, quite askew,
Looks like it's pondering, 'What's my cue?'

Raindrops of glitter fell from the sky,
As cousin Tim made the sprinkles fly.
The walls, the floor, now all a swirl,
Of giggles and paint, what a wild whirl!

With every stroke, we laughed aloud,
A masterpiece made, we're feeling proud.
A memory framed, not just for show,
In our hearts, this joy will glow.

Threading Memories Through Time

Each ornament tells a tale so grand,
An old sock puppet, lost in the sand.
Grandpa's mustache, a twist of yarn,
Brought back the laughs with festive charm.

Cookie cutter shapes, a mixed-up crew,
Yes, that's a tree, or is it a shoe?
The cupcakes sing, "We're all part of this!"
Uncle Bob squished one, can you believe this?

Threads of laughter weave through the night,
As cousins giggle, hearts feeling light.
A braided record of mischief and cheer,
With every stitch, we hold memories dear.

So hang the stories, let them out,
With every giggle, we twist and shout.
In this web of joy, we all belong,
A tapestry rich, where we sing our song.

Illuminations of Winter Tales

Glowing lights blink like a playful tease,
While the cat chases shadows with ease.
A snowman with sunglasses is quite a sight,
As laughter erupts in the chilly night.

The stockings filled with candy canes,
Whispers of joy entwined with refrains.
Silly hats worn a touch too tight,
Family snapshots bring such delight!

The cookies on plates, all gone in a flash,
While Uncle's rants turn into a clash.
The holiday tunes spinning in the air,
Dance like nobody's watching — no reason to care!

So let these moments swirl and sway,
Silly and bright, in the festive play.
Illuminate hearts with laughter's embrace,
In this winter wonder, we find our place.

Harmony in Holiday Colors

Deck the halls with colors bright,
Tinsel dances in the light.
Ornaments hang, what a sight,
Even the cat's in festive fright!

Reindeer socks, what a choice,
Gingerbread men, they rejoice.
Children giggle, all have a voice,
As Santa's sleigh makes its noise.

Lights that blink in wild array,
Magic fills the joyful sway.
Every corner sings today,
Even Grandpa's beard turned gray!

Laughter echoes through the night,
Mistletoe hung, a funny plight.
Kisses stolen, oh what a bite,
Season's greetings, pure delight!

The Warmth Within the Green

Underneath the tree so bright,
Presents stacked with all their might.
Dad's snoring, what a sight,
Dreaming of cookies in the night.

Lights are twinkling, all aglow,
Sisters bicker 'bout the bow.
Mom just laughs, she's in the flow,
While Grandpa tries to steal the show.

Elf hats placed on every head,
Poor Fido feels underfed.
Slippers worn, but not in red,
As bedtime stories must be read.

The fireplace crackles, warmth it lends,
Family gathers, love transcends.
With laughter shared, it never ends,
In silly hats, we are all friends!

Shadows of Festive Delight

In the evening, shadows creep,
But candles glow, and laughter leaps.
Cookies crumbed, oh what a heap,
While kids in sugar dreams do sleep.

The star atop, slightly askew,
Uncle Bob claims he's the glue.
He sticks to jokes like they're true,
With punchlines aimed at me and you.

Snowflakes swirl, a chilly plight,
But inside, it's cozy and bright.
A dance-off starts, what a sight!
As grandmas shuffle with delight.

With cards and games scattered 'round,
And laughter shared, a merry sound.
We find a joy that knows no bound,
In every hug and sight profound.

Whispers of Winter's Embrace

Winter whispers in the air,
Snowflakes tumble without a care.
Hot cocoa served, a chocolate flare,
As marshmallows dance without a scare.

Bells are jingling, soft and sweet,
Laughter echoes, a joyful beat.
The puppy plays with twinkling feet,
And finds the ornaments to greet.

Grandma's cookies, there's no doubt,
A secret recipe she'll shout.
But burned ones 'neath the tree, no clout,
Fly off the plate, watch them pout.

With scarves wrapped tight, the carols start,
Family gathers, close to heart.
These moments captured, a vital part,
Of winter's magic, we play our part!

A Sprig of Nostalgia

The bauble spilled its stories bright,
Of cat chasing lights in the night.
Grandma's cookies with sprinkles on top,
A sneaky bite made the laughter pop.

Uncle Fred danced with a tree on his head,
While Aunt Sue hid the gift under her bed.
The tinsel tangled in everyone's hair,
As we giggled at chaos that filled the air.

A snowman built from socks and a hat,
Skewed and lopsided, a true work of scat.
With each ornament hung, a chuckle we'd share,
Memories wrapped in holiday flair.

Candles flicker with a warm, silly glow,
While the dog thinks the tree's a new toy, oh no!
We gather 'round for cheers and for fun,
In the spirit of laughter, the loveliest run.

Secrets Wrapped in Ribbons

Under the tree, boxes piled high,
With secrets inside that make us all sigh.
Ribbons and bows hiding raucous delight,
As stories unfold on a magical night.

A grandpa who snores while the kids take the stage,
Reciting their lines with whimsical rage.
Mittens wrapped up with a note: 'Not for you!'
Whispers of laughter from each little crew.

The dog unwrapped his own special toy,
And made it his mission to ravage with joy.
While elves on the shelves watched the kitty's spree,
Snickering softly at their own merry glee.

Each package a puzzle, each gift a surprise,
As we share out the giggles and widen our eyes.
With moments like these, bland days drift away,
In the laughter of secrets, we choose to stay.

Whispers of Evergreen

Beneath the boughs of the evergreen's cheer,
We'd whisper our wishes to the tree so near.
Its needles held stories of seasons gone past,
As we laughed about how all the ornaments cast.

The star on top leaned a tad to the right,
While grandma swore it looked just out of sight.
With popcorn strings tangled and horns made from cups,
We sang silly carols till the grown-ups gave up.

A cat leapt up high, snagging garland with glee,
Leaving mischief and giggles under the tree.
Our family chaos turned sweet holiday lore,
As we danced and we spun on the slick kitchen floor.

With each ornament hung, a chuckle we'd find,
Twinkles and tinsel forever entwined.
In whispers of evergreen, laughter takes flight,
A holiday saga 'neath stars shining bright.

Ornaments of Memory

Each ornament tells a story, you see,
Of toothpaste snowmen crafted with glee.
A reindeer who waddled, with one funny leg,
And mismatched socks wrapped around the egg.

The chaos of wrapping paper piled high,
While kids climbed the tree, oh my, oh my!
With mugs filled with cocoa, laughter in the air,
As each seen and unseen sparked joy everywhere.

A cousin who sneezed in the midst of a song,
And Aunt Linda's tales of how Christmas went wrong.
While the cat launched an attack on the feast,
Leaving a scene that could make laughter increase.

Under bright lights, our memories weave,
Stories of chaos, we choose to believe.
In ornaments glowing, our smiles take flight,
In this funny mish-mash, our hearts feel so light.

A Pine-Scented Dream

In a corner, a squirrel with flair,
Stole the tinsel, oh what a scare!
He danced on a branch, quite a sight,
While the cat plotted a daring bite.

The lights twinkled, a colorful show,
But one bulb winked, said, "Oh no, no!"
A flicker of laughter filled the room,
As dad tripped over the vacuum's zoom.

A candy cane battle commenced at last,
With giggles and shouts, oh what a blast!
Mom's laughter echoed, the cookies flew,
Leaving crumbs for the mice, one or two.

Under the tree, in cozy heaps,
All the pets gathered, silent peeps.
While the humans exchanged their gifts,
The ham stole the show with its zesty twists.

Glittering Secrets Above

Up above, the ornaments wink,
Whispering secrets as we all think.
A wise old owl perched on high,
Rolling his eyes as he watched the pie.

A kitten jumped, caught in the glow,
Chasing a sparkle, putting on a show.
The dog barked loudly, tripped on the rug,
And bumped the tree, a festive tug.

Mom said, "Careful! Don't touch that flair!"
But the toddler giggled, a bit unaware.
He reached for a light, let out a squeak,
The tree swayed gently, quite unique.

As snowflakes danced on the window pane,
The laughter and joy, like a sweet champagne.
With every mishap, not one could frown,
For memories made are the best around.

The Star's Silent Watch

Atop the tree, the star held tight,
Watching the chaos with patient delight.
The kids spun around, arms open wide,
Pretending to fly on a winter ride.

An elf with a hat, too big to wear,
Danced round the room, without a care.
He slipped on some ribbons, down he went,
Creating a mess, the laughter spent.

As cookies were baked, the flour flew,
A nice little cloud, quite white and new.
The dog licked the bowl, such a good boy,
While the kids planned a heist, oh what joy!

The star twinkled brightly, a cheerleader true,
For all the wild wonders that these kids do.
With every giggle, and silly mistake,
The warmth of this season was theirs to take.

Beneath the Boughs

Beneath the boughs, a treasure chest,
Filled with surprises, a holiday quest.
The cat found a ribbon, a snatch and a dash,
Suddenly tangled, a colorful clash.

The kids crept slowly, with stealthy delight,
Imitating ninjas, ready for flight.
But slipped on a gift, wrapped up with care,
Sending everyone rolling, a laughter affair.

A feast laid out, with goodies galore,
The dog sneaked a cookie, wanting more.
While the family giggled, the chaos spilled,
With each little moment, their hearts were filled.

So here in the warmth, with stories to share,
Under the tree, joy was everywhere.
For laughter and love, that's what we see,
Magic resides in all of us, carefree.

The Candle's Quiet Glow

A candle flickers, oh what a sight,
Stands on the table, feeling quite bright.
It sways and dances, making a show,
"Watch me, I'm magic!" it seems to crow.

The cat leaps up, a stealthy game,
Paws on the table, oh what a shame!
Knocks over cookies, down they all go,
The candle just giggles, "What a fine show!"

Aunt Marge walks in, with a giant cake,
"I hope that stays there! For goodness' sake!"
The candle winks, as if to bestow,
"Don't worry dear Marge, I'm all set to glow!"

Later we laugh, oh what a night,
With crumbs on our shirts and our hearts so light.
The candle is tired, its work now slow,
And winks at the chaos, in the soft, warm glow.

Secrets of the Ornamented Sphere

An ornament shimmered, with secrets so bright,
It whispered to fir-trees, all through the night.
"I've seen many things, oh yes I can tell,
Of snowflakes and laughter, and even a bell!"

Uncle Joe stumbles, his drink in his hand,
"What's that you're saying? I don't understand!"
The bulb shakes with laughter, a chuckle, a twirl,
"Never mind, my friend, come give this a whirl!"

The children come close, their eyes all aglow,
They reach for the secrets, just waiting to show.
With tales of the past, the joy and the cheer,
The ornament chuckles, "You've nothing to fear!"

At the end of the night, with the clock striking late,
The sphere grins wide, feeling quite great.
Its giggle still lingers, as dreams softly flow,
Now tucked in the branches, where secrets still grow!

Frosted Dreams by Firelight

Frosted windows, a magical sight,
The fire crackles, bringing such light.
Marshmallows roasting, oh what a blast,
Time for some laughter, and good cheer, at last!

Grandpa starts telling tales from his youth,
Of snowball fights, and the toothless truth.
The flames dance higher, with sparks flying bright,
A story ensues, turning wrongs into right!

The pets all listen, ears perked up high,
Wondering 'what next?' as the sparks zoom by.
"Watch me catch one!" the pup starts to leap,
Aiming for magic, not knowing it's sleep!

Through laughter and warmth, the night drifts along,
Embrace the silly, as we sing our song.
Frosted dreams linger, with joy taking flight,
By the fire's warm glow, all feels just right.

Tales from a Holiday Haven

In the corner sits, the old holiday chair,
With cushions and stories that linger in air.
"I'm the king of comfort, come join me and sit!"
The cat rolls her eyes, "Get up, you old git!"

The stockings hang low, all stuffed with delight,
A game of 'find out' is played every night.
With candy canes poking, and giggles in spree,
"What's hiding in there? Oh, look! It's me!"

A snowman is built, though it leans to the side,
With a carrot for nose, and such winter pride.
"Hey, my hat's too big!" it shouts with a grin,
As kids roll on snow, with laughter within.

From cookies to chaos, this sanctuary glows,
With mirth and with magic, each moment bestows.
A haven of cheer, where all are embraced,
In this funny realm, our smiles interlaced!

Beneath the Glittering Attire

Under the sparkle, cats lay in wait,
Pouncing on ornaments—oh, what a fate!
Tinsel tangles in fuzzy paws tight,
While we laugh softly, what a silly sight!

Cookies go missing, but crumbs lead the way,
Who could have nibbled on our festive tray?
The dog winks at me, a guilty delight,
While we stuff our bellies with all that feels right!

The lights flicker wildly, a dance of pure glee,
As Uncle Joe trips, oh dear, can it be?
He lands on the tree, our decorations in tow,
We laugh and we cheer, what a glorious show!

So gather around, with laughter and cheer,
These moments we treasure, year after year.
With joy like confetti, we'll always be found,
Beneath the glittering attire, love's all around!

The Festive Fables

Once upon a time, a squirrel wore a hat,
He stole all the nuts, how about that?
The children all giggled as he dashed away,
Chasing a legend from an old holiday!

The snowman wobbled, a tip and a sway,
With a carrot nose slipping, a grand cabaret!
He danced through the night, what a sight to behold,
With laughter and snowflakes, his story unfolded!

Grandpa's yawn echoed, the clock struck a chime,
He told the best jokes, bending space-time!
With each silly story, we snorted with glee,
The festive fables forever will be!

So toast to the moments we share near the fire,
With every crackle, our spirits climb higher.
Wrapped in the laughter, we feel so alive,
In whimsical tales, our hearts truly thrive!

Captured Moments of Joy

Photos galore in our holiday spree,
Gramps with a beard, looks like Santa, you see!
Mom tries to juggle, the cookies take flight,
While we snap the pic, what a comical sight!

Siblings in chaos, a glorious show,
Baking mishaps with frosting like snow.
The cat licks the batter, oh my dear friend,
Captured moments of joy, on them we depend!

The tree's the backdrop for many a pose,
With goofy expressions and matching clothes.
Later we'll chuckle, retelling the fun,
As another Christmas brings memories spun!

So gather your laughter, and hold it quite tight,
These captured moments make everything right.
With each snapshot, we savor the glee,
In laughter and love, we're forever carefree!

Chronology of the Season

In early December, the lights go up bright,
Neighbors compete in a dazzling sight.
Gingerbread houses take shape and flare,
Yet, who can resist frosting everywhere?

Mid-month reveals a big elf's parade,
When silly mishaps in socks are displayed.
Kids sing out loud, with voices all wrong,
A chorus of giggles, our hearts sing along!

As parties unfold, the punch spills with cheer,
We dance like mad fools while munching on beer.
Grandma tells stories, with a wink and a grin,
About mischief we made while she took a spin!

So mark down the days, let the nonsense commence,
In the chronology of laughter, there's no recompense.
For the memories made will forever remain,
As we dance through the season, again and again!

Whispers of Evergreen

In the corner, the cat plays,
Chasing shadows in a daze.
Tinsel stuck to his fur,
He prances, quite unsure.

Pine cones in a brawl,
Rolling 'neath the wall.
They giggle as they roll,
Nature's jest at pole.

Socks hanging, full of cheer,
Spilling secrets, oh so near.
They whisper late at night,
Hoping for a playful bite.

A squirrel peeks from a branch,
Wonders if he'll get a chance.
To nibble on sweet candy,
Now that would be quite dandy!

Ornamented Memories

A bulb flickers, green then red,
Does it know we all just fled?
The dog chewed through the light,
Now it looks like a fright!

Grandma's face with a grin,
As she tries to spin.
A scarf stuck on her nose,
A fashion faux pas, I suppose!

The elf on the shelf took a dive,
Land on the cake? He feels alive!
We laughed till we cried,
That frosting was well fried!

A gingerbread man, oh so bold,
Claimed he could turn to gold!
But once he took a bite,
He crumbled in sheer fright!

The Star's Secret Song

High above, the star did hum,
Making the whole tree go numb.
It sang of epic flights,
And dazzling holiday sights.

But one night it lost its tune,
Flashing bright like a cartoon.
The ornaments started to dance,
Caught up in this merry trance!

The candy canes shuffled too,
In a blend of old and new.
As garlands tried to swing low,
Creating quite the flashy show!

We bowed with laughter grand,
Our festive, joyful band.
So much cheer in the night,
All thanks to that star's delight!

Garlands of Goodwill

The garlands giggle in a row,
Twisting tales, putting on a show.
They trip and tangle, oh my dear,
Creating chaos, spreading cheer!

A mouse frolics with delight,
Running left, then to the right.
He tugs a bow, what a mess,
The tree now looks in distress!

The lights start to bob and weave,
As if they're trying to deceive.
The ornaments begin to sway,
Caught in the frolic of play.

With each chuckle, the night grows bright,
Filled with warmth and pure delight.
So here's to fun, may it stay,
In quirky, sparkling, festive play!

The Magic of December Nights

In a corner, a gnome in a hat,
Dreams of cheese—imagine that!
Twinkling lights, they dance and jig,
Can a snowman really do the wig?

Santa's reindeer, stuck in a tree,
Singing carols, oh so free!
The ornaments chuckle, round and bright,
Who knew that they could take to flight?

A cat on a branch, with a curious stare,
Paws and tinsel in a playful scare.
When the gifts start to rattle and roll,
Who will be crowned the wrapping paper troll?

Frosty sips cocoa, a mischievous grin,
Chasing the kids, oh, where to begin?
At dawn they'll find, with giggles galore,
The magic of nights that they'll all adore!

Tales Hidden in the Tinsel

Beneath the branches, a dog made of fluff,
Gnawing on ribbons, oh, isn't that tough?
A rocking horse whispers, "Let's take a ride!"
While a fairy is lost in a candy cane slide.

Garland giggles as they wrap around tight,
"Don't pull us too hard, we're reaching new heights!"
Snowflakes tumble, soft and misplaced,
Amidst all the laughter, nobody's graced.

A squirrel pops in for a festive chat,
Asking the tree if it's really that fat.
Gifts piled high, what secrets they hide,
"Open me first!" says the teddy with pride.

As Christmas morn arrives with delight,
Chaos erupts in the soft morning light.
With tinsel all tangled and cookies astray,
Who knew the holidays could be so cliché?

Pine-Coned Memories

Under the tree, a kitten so spry,
Chasing the branches as time passes by.
Pinecones gather to share silly jokes,
While elves in the corner trade stories of blokes.

A Santa sock filled with mismatched pairs,
Looking for warmth, oh, how it stares!
A sock puppet battle breaks out with cheer,
"Who needs a foot when we've got a rear?"

The lights shimmer brightly, a disco ball flare,
As mistletoe whispers, "Don't you dare care!"
Candy canes giggle at gingerbread men,
Silly food fights erupt now and then.

December nights filled with silliness and glee,
Where laughter is wrapped, just like gifts on a spree.
Pine-coned memories, forever they'll sow,
In the heart of the tree, where all the fun flows!

The Lullaby of Lowly Lights

In the stillness, a garland hums,
Lullabies sung by the beat of drums.
A mouse in a thimble, oh what a sight,
Drumming on cookies, into the night.

Each bulb a story, each flicker a cheer,
Piggybacks forming among holiday beer.
With giggles and wiggles, all wrapped in cheer,
A sloth in the corner feels perfectly clear.

A snow globe shakes, releasing a dance,
As the lights twist and turn—what a strange chance!
Up on the top, a star looks down low,
"It's a party up here! Come join the show!"

At the end of the night, they all share a grin,
With whispers of joy and warmth from within.
The lullaby sings, in the glow so bright,
As they dream of the fun found in December nights!

Stories Swaddled in Satin

Beneath the sparkly lights so bright,
Old ornaments squabble, what a sight!
They blush in gold, they twirl in glee,
"Last year's mishap? That's not me!"

Tinsel fights with a rogue pinecone,
"You think you're fancy, all on your own!"
As ribbons giggle and bows take flight,
"Let's wrap this up before it's night!"

A cat conspirator, on stealthy paws,
Leaps up with joy, defying the laws.
"Watch your baubles!" echoes through the air,
As chaos unfolds without a care.

At last, they settle, the peace is near,
With stories woven in laughs and cheer.
Each sparkle having a secret comrade,
In this grand saga that we've all made.

Pinecone Chronicles

Gather round, all the pinecones said,
"We've seen it all, come grab a thread!"
With squirrelly tales of chestnut heists,
They chuckle at cats who missed their flights.

One proudly boasts of a birdhouse raid,
While others chime in, unafraid.
"Oh, the humans don't hide their snacks too well!
What a glorious fiesta! You can't quite tell!"

They dance on branches to jingling sounds,
While twinkling lights sway all around.
"Let's create mischief, no need to beg!
We'll knock down this tree with a boisterous leg!"

As night descends, they sing their tune,
With laughter echoing beneath the moon.
A chorus of chaos, of fun and cheer,
Pinecone Chronicles, a festive sphere.

Lanterns of Yesteryear

Remember when Mom baked pies galore?
The kids would sneak some, always wanting more.
But the cat found a way to steal the show,
Knocking thrice before the oven's glow.

Lanterns flicker with mischief and glee,
Recounting wild stories, just you and me.
"I swear that one's from Uncle Joe's thrift shop,
It lights up yelling when you let it drop!"

In the corner, an elf is stuck on a tree,
Some help him down, but not for free!
"Join us in laughter, come take a seat,
We'll tell you of mishaps and chocolate treats!"

As we huddle close, our hearts align,
Old lanterns dance with a quirky shine.
In the mix of whimsy, we raise a cheer,
For every mishap, we hold oh so dear.

Silent Nights, Bright Memories

In quiet corners, whispers arise,
Of fuzzy socks and childhood pies.
"Did you see the cat with a glorious leap?"
As memories twirl, we all just peep.

A snowman outside looks quite confused,
With a carrot nose that seems rather bruised.
"Did you hear the snowball that got away?
It nearly took out Grandma's shawl today!"

Cookies enchanted with sprinkles galore,
Mysteriously vanish, leaving us poor.
"What happened to dinner? It vanished, you see!"
While uncles just giggled, clutching their tea.

As stories we weave, through laughter we share,
Silent nights filled with joy in the air.
In bright memories captured, we find delight,
Merriment shines in the glow of the night.

A Journey of Holiday Spirits

A reindeer with a funny grin,
Stole Santa's hat, now where to begin?
The elves are chasing, oh what a sight,
As he prances around, full of delight.

Frosty the snowman, what a strange sight,
He danced with the kids until the midnight light.
With carrot nose wiggling, he slipped on the ice,
Landed in snowbanks, not so precise!

Grandma's cookies are gone in a blink,
The dog caught the scent and no time to think.
He gobbled them up, left crumbs everywhere,
Next year we'll hide them—so he won't dare!

The ornaments chatter while hanging in place,
Whispering secrets of the family grace.
One said, "Remember the cat's great leap?"
But quickly, they shushed, now no one can sleep!

Reflections in Silver and Gold

The tinsel shimmered, blinding the eye,
And one little child thought he could fly.
He climbed up the tree like a squirrel with flair,
Just for a moment—then down in despair!

Uncle Joe tried to hang the lights right,
But tangled them up in a comical fight.
His pants got caught, what a sight to behold,
"Who needs a ladder?" he laughed, brave and bold.

The star on the top looks a bit out of place,
It wobbled and swayed like it's doing a race.
A sprinkle of glitter, a sprinkle of fun,
Can't wait to see what happens when it's done!

As we snack on the treats laid out on the floor,
The puppy sneaks in, oh what a score!
With crumbs on his snout, he dashes away,
Guess he's the winner of this holiday!

Stardust and Shadows

Under the tree, a mystery unfolds,
Wrapped up in paper, a treasure that holds.
But oh what a blunder, the gifts went astray,
And socks filled with candy, all for display!

The twinkling lights are having a feud,
One sparkles bright while the other is rude.
They taunt each other with colors so bold,
"Who needs a Christmas story?" they chide and scold.

The cat in the corner, so whimsically sly,
Caught the garland's glimmer from way up high.
With a leap and a pounce, she managed to swing,
Now cats 'n' tinsel is quite the thing!

As snowflakes twirl down from skies so wide,
The snowmen are laughing, they just can't hide.
A hat made of lettuce, a nose that's a bean,
Now who's looking stylish? It's quite the scene!

Journeys Through the Jingle

Each jingle bell rings with a quirky sound,
As the buggy old carolers stroll all around.
One lost his shoe, oh what a fuss,
Now they're all singing, 'Who's driving this bus?'

The cookies are dancing, on plates they prance,
Santa's belly giggles as he joins in the dance.
"Pass me the frosting, oh what a treat!"
While sprinkles are flying   oh, isn't this neat?

Grandpa in reindeer antlers, quite the sight,
Giggling like a child, he's feeling just right.
He says, "My dear friends, 'tis the season to cheer,"
And promptly fell asleep with a mug of cold beer!

With laughter and joy scattered all 'round,
We gather together, our hearts intertwined.
In crazy traditions and moments of glee,
We cherish the fun—just like you and me!

Under the Glittering Canopy

Under the lights that twinkle bright,
A cat takes flight, what a silly sight!
Tinsel and bows dance all around,
As laughter rings, our joy is found.

Cookies misplaced, on the table they sit,
Our dog stole the tray; now he's having a fit!
Mom's all aglow, but the fudge is now gone,
Tommy insists, it's all squirrels' fault, come dawn.

A star on top, lopsided and proud,
Gramps yells 'It's perfect!' to the silent crowd.
We gather close, with puns in the air,
This festive chaos, we can't help but share.

With giggles and cheer, we sing off-key,
Bells that clang, what a jolly spree!
In our silly world, where mishaps abound,
Love wraps us up, joyously wound.

The Harvest of Hope

On the first of December, we gather at noon,
With gloves on our hands, we're singing a tune.
Each ornament hung, with a story to tell,
Even Grandma's yarn ball has some tales to sell.

Uncle Joe trips, nearly topples the chair,
But insists he was dancing, all flashy and rare.
The fruitcake's survived, though it's hard as a rock,
We all take a slice—then a loud, stunned shock!

Kids in their PJs, eyes wide as they peek,
At the pile of gifts, oh, what a unique streak!
The wrapping is shiny, but what's it all mean?
A sock for the dog? What a riotous scene!

In the midst of our giggles, a moment appears,
Where we raise merry toast, and all share our cheers.
With laughter to share, and cookies galore,
We harvest the hope that we cherish and adore.

Enchanted Evenings

In the glow of the night, the magic is here,
A mishap with lights, igniting some cheer.
As the bulb explodes, it gives quite a fright,
But we're all doubling over, it's quite the delight!

The elves in the corner tangle in bows,
Wrapping each other like presents, who knows?
With a wink and a grin, they make quite a scene,
In our cozy chaos, life's a sweet dream.

Choco balls roll from the kitchen with ease,
Puppies parade, stealing crumbs, what a tease!
A ruckus resounds as the reindeer dance by,
Underneath all the laughter, a glimmering sky.

As we cozy on up, in our jammies we glide,
Telling tall tales, no secret to hide.
Enchanted these evenings, with joy and some snacks,
Together we thrive, as we all share the laughs.

Evergreen Echoes

In a forest of fluff, where needles do shed,
Our tree stands proud, with a hat on its head.
Enrico the squirrel, tail high with delight,
Is scaring the dog with his antics tonight.

The popcorn garland, a treat much too sweet,
Turns dinner-time fun into a howl and retreat.
Mom yells, 'Don't eat it!' every time they try,
As we watch them succeed, with twinkles in eye.

A dance in the kitchen, the family's so bold,
Uncle Bob's two-step is a sight to behold!
With eggnog in hand, we stumble and sway,
In this merry circus, our cares float away.

Echoes of laughter ring clear through the cheer,
As we toast to the moments that bring us all near.
With evergreen joy, and our funny routine,
We celebrate life, in our holiday scene.

Milton Keynes UK
Ingram Content Group UK Ltd.
UKHW030750121124
451094UK00013B/822